GOD
and a
Mouse
"Topolito"

This book is dedicated
to Sister M. Rosario Martinez
and to all those
who love little things...

GOD
and a
Mouse

a festival of reflective jubilation

Illustrated by De Grazia
Words by Sister M. Angela, O.S.B.

Published by
Benedictine Sisters
3888 Paducah Drive
San Diego, California 92117

Illustrations created especially for this book, and
are reproduced with special permission of the
De Grazia Gallery In The Sun,
6300 North Swan, Tucson, Arizona.

First Printing, 1972
Second Printing, 1976
Third Printing, 1977
Fourth Printing, 1979
Fifth Printing, 1980
Sixth Printing, 1983
Seventh Printing, 1985

Library of Congress
Catalog Card Number 72-84198

ISBN 0-913180-01-7

at first glance this may appear
rather simple – it's supposed to be
that way for the life of a mouse
is not complicated.

his whole life is full of traps,
yet he bears the world no grudge.
a small mouse is too big to carry a
chip on his shoulder. he is a
sensitive creature and bears
empathy for the world.

there is a funny-side to life and a
serious-side. either side alone,
exclusive of the other, can be
man's biggest trap.

if you try to make the best out of
life you will see how great it is
. . . and maybe be surprised . . .
how much the world needs *you!*

Dios mio,

my home is small . . .
the door, it is always open.
do not knock – You are always welcome
                to come in.

> **Dios mio —**
> > **stay**
> > **with me . . .**

Dios mio,

the floor is drafty.
my feet are aching . . .
the cat is wont to chase me
    the whole day long.
why did You make for me
    such a long tail?
must i run in order to live?

      Dios mio —

         hold me
         in Your hand . . .

Dios mio,

i want to sing to You
but my voice is weak . . .
You give me such a 'squeek'
. . . but . . . i sing anyway . . .

> *Dios mio —*
>> *You are*
>> *smiling . . .*

Dios mio,

i am hungry . . .
the cheese is good . . . but . . .
    it would taste better
    if not always served in a trap!

       Dios mio —
           call me
           to Your table . . .

Dios mio,

the church is quiet.
i have plenty of room in the pew.
i see You ... and You see me.

> **Dios mio —**
>> *we are*
>> *happy ...*

no more numbers...

Dios mio,

the raindrops are big today.
i run for shelter in the deep grass
        and fall asleep . . .
i dream of You.

> *Dios mio* —
>
>   *cover*
>   *me . . .*

Dios mio,

i am lonely . . .
do You have time to play
    with me?
    let us run
    in the freedom of the field.

          Dios mio —
               wait
               for me . . .

Dios mio,

the flowers smell nice.
the weeds, they are good too.
each one has its own place
        to grow in the ground.
it is beautiful.

> ***Dios mio —***
>   *plant me*
>   *in Your heart . . .*

Dios mio,

thank you for my friend.
he has a kind heart
and teaches me how to trust.

> **Dios mio —**
> **Your eyes**
> **have tears . . .**

Dios mio,

i run to the crushed leaves.
they are hurt when they fall
    from the trees.
. . . but i try to comfort them.

> *Dios mio —*
>   *heal them*
>   *before winter . . .*

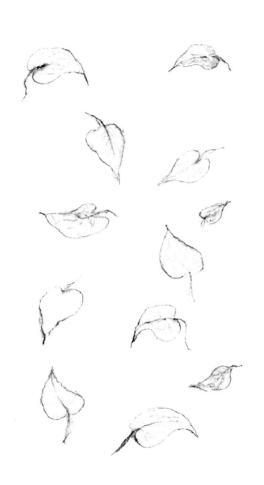

Dios mio,

the world is full of regrets.
the people sigh and scuff
    their feet on the sidewalk.
i hide in the alley.
maybe it is better there . . .
    no, . . . i think it is best
    to face the world.

                Dios mio —
                    give
                    them hope . . .

Dios mio,

the birds have a hard time
finding food today.
i offer them my cheese.
    maybe . . . they will eat it.

            Dios mio —
                  feed
                  the hungry . . .

Dios mio,

the stars are so small.
i want to see them closer
        but You put them too deep
        in the sky.

                    Dios mio —
                            lift me
                            up . . .

Dios mio,

the morning dew is cold on my feet.
i help the little violets open their petals
and . . . jump up
     to kiss the dandelions.
they like it . . .

       Dios mio —

         let all the world
         have a
         "good morning" . . .

Dios mio,

why do the children run
when they see me coming?
i want to make friends with them
    but they run away.

> *Dios mio* —
>> *never let me*
>> *run away from what*
>> *i don't understand . . .*

Dios mio,

the sun is like a big fire
in the sky. it is hot and
the cat is crabby.
i best stay
        in my house today.

                Dios mio —
                        make some shade
                        for the people . . .

Dios mio,

today i got lost in the cornfield.
i cried amid the giant stalks
because i was afraid.
    they understood my weakness
and said it was not wrong to cry.
sometimes it is better to cry,
    than not to cry.

          Dios mio —

            ***help the people
            who cannot find
            themselves . . .***

Dios mio,

food is scarce yet
i have gathered many crumbs today.
i will give them to those
who are poorer than me.

> *Dios mio —*
>> *the poor*
>> *are grateful*
>> *for gifts . . .*

Dios mio,

my heart is pounding.
the people have placed for me
many traps tonight.
they want to catch me
        not alive – but dead!

                Dios mio —
                        raise
                        the dead . . .

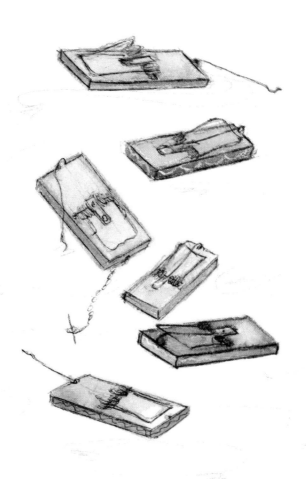

Dios mio,

today the world is laughing.
i can feel the ground shake.
i try smiling at the cat,
      maybe . . . he will smile
      back at me . . .

                ***Dios mio* —**
                    turn enemies
                    into friends . . .

Dios mio,

i have important question.
cages . . . they are to keep something in
            or keep something out?
i look and see if lock
is on inside or outside.
        maybe someday
        nobody need cages.

                Dios mio —
                        teach the world
                        discernment . . .

Dios mio,

today i go to birthday party.
we have good time . . .
sing 'happy birthday' song
        and give presents.
why wait til birthday to sing song
and give gift . . . maybe person need
party in heart 'now.'

> *Dios mio —*
>> *send invitations . . .*

Dios mio,

today i watch sunset.
oh . . . soooo beautiful. – i clap hands.
do for me again. i like to watch You.
    maybe tomorrow
    people see nice colors too.

        Dios mio —
            show them
            bright side of life . . .

Walker Lithocraft • Tucson, Arizo